LOFTHOUSE
CHILDHOOD
MEMORIES
OF
A
NIDDERDALE
VILLAGE

By
CHRISTINE MARY COURT (NÉE EGLIN)

Edited by
JOHN WATMOUGH

Published in 2018 by:
John Watmough
46, Ainsty Road
Wetherby
West Yorkshire
LS22 7QS
john.watmough@gmail.com

ISBN 978-1-5272-2511-4

Map © Ordnance Survey

Front cover: Fountains Farm
with Christine outside the front gate.

Inside rear cover: Scar House Reservoir.

Rear cover: Lofthouse village.

Designed and printed by:
A1 Press (Sherburn in Elmet) Ltd.
01937 588750
www.a1press.co.uk

INTRODUCTION

This booklet contains the childhood memories of Christine Mary Court who grew up during the 1940's living at Fountains Farm in the village of Lofthouse, Upper Nidderdale, Yorkshire. Christine was the second daughter of William Gilbert and Isabella (Cissie) Eglin. Her eleven-years older sister Judith was my mother. The Eglin's had previously farmed two miles further up the dale at Haver Close until 1937.

Christine was born on 26th December 1937 and passed away on 17th August 2017 aged 79 years. After leaving Lofthouse, Christine moved with her parents to a farm in Earby, near Skipton. On leaving school she took a job at Barnoldswick Post Office. In 1957 she became a police officer and was based in Keighley. She then joined the Northern Rhodesian Police Force, a branch of the then British South African Police Force, in Northern Rhodesia (now Zambia) in 1960. There she married a South African, and moved to Hillcrest in Kwa Zulu Natal, where daughter Judy and son Andrew were born. There she was the chief Librarian of Hillcrest Library for many years, overseeing the building of the new library in the seventies. Christine's later years were spent in Benoni, a few miles east of Johannesburg. There she was the Personal Assistant of two different CEO's of large companies until she retired. Christine loved to paint and specialised in water colours – creating wonderful renderings of the places she visited around the world from photographs she had taken. She also played lawn bowls and led quite an active social life until months before her passing. Right until her death she received copies of The Dalesman and read anything and everything on Yorkshire voraciously – still calling Yorkshire "home" even after nearly fifty years living abroad.

Christine started writing her memories around 1988 and later commenced editing them, but sadly passed away whilst she was undertaking the task. I am pleased to have been given the opportunity to finish them. Christine had lent me a copy to read when I visited her in 2015. It quickly became apparent her recollections and anecdotes would provide a small but valuable contribution to the cultural heritage of a Yorkshire dales village. There are also interesting observations of how the Second World War affected life in Lofthouse. I can reveal there has already been a favourable reaction following the publication of extracts on social media. I am therefore grateful to my cousin Judy Stephan, who now lives in Canada, for agreeing to send me her mother's memories and allow them to reach a wider audience.

Some of the names have been omitted from my auntie's original text and a few of the terms and expressions used have also been changed as they are no longer appropriate in this day and age. As Christine herself writes, daily life was very different from that of today's society!

On a personal note, I spent nearly three years living on my grandparent's farm at Earby, so some of the recollections strike a chord. I can recall haytime on a hot summers day with a picnic from cloth covered wicker baskets and lukewarm tea poured from quart-sized brown bottles. Also the days spent building dams across becks, roaming the fields, playing in barns and riding on grandad's tractor.

I especially want to thank my cousin Judy for her assistance with her mother's memories. Also Christine's cousin Elizabeth Mason for her advice, contacts, support and help with checking names and dates.

In addition, I wish to acknowledge and thank the following: Michelle Clare, Dinah Lee, Robert Light, Elizabeth Simpson and John Taylor.

Finally, feedback or comments from any reader who remembers Christine are welcome.

John Watmough (July 2018)

Since Christine's Memories first appeared in 2018, many appreciative comments from readers have been received, including several who knew her. I am very grateful to everyone who requested copies and the numerous shops and other outlets who stocked the booklet. This has prompted me to order a reprint. Feedback drew attention to a couple incorrect names in the text and these have been amended.

John Watmough (March 2019)

BIBLIOGRAPHY AND FURTHER READING

Jennings, B. (1992) A History of Nidderdale 3rd ed. The Nidderdale History Group: Pateley Bridge.

Lee, D. (n/d) Middlesmoor – a stone's-throw from heaven.

Lofthouse Conservation Area Character Appraisal (2010) Harrogate Borough Council. [Internet], https://www.nidderdaleaonb.org.uk/ckfinder/userfiles/files/Planning/CAA_Lofthouse.pdf

Moody, J. (2014) Traces of Nidderdale in 40 years and 40 objects: stories of the museum. Pateley Bridge, North Yorkshire: Nidderdale Museum Society.

Nidderdale: Fountain's Abbey, Ripon & Pateley Bridge: the essential map for outdoor activities (2013) Map, Edition B2. Series: OS explorer map; 298. Southampton: Ordnance Survey.

People and Places: Memories of Upper Nidderdale (2008) Upper Nidderdale Local History Group.

Upper Nidderdale Landscape Partnership.[Internet], http://uppernidderdale.org.uk/

LOFTHOUSE - THE VILLAGE, OUR FARM
AND PEOPLE I REMEMBER

Lofthouse is a small village situated in the Yorkshire Dales on the banks of the River Nidd in Upper Nidderdale. The houses were built from grey Pennine stone, the exception being several semi-detached council houses which were covered in what was known as "pebble dash." I had friends who lived in these houses and was always envious of them. Heaven knows why, because I was born and brought up in a large house which faced the village square. This was Fountains Farm (though it is no longer a farmhouse) named after the drinking fountain which stands in front of it. The farmhouse not only had five bedrooms and an upstairs bathroom, but also a large kitchen, dairy, living room and what dad, William Gilbert Eglin (always known as Gilbert), used to refer to as the "parlour," plus it had a cottage tacked onto the end. The stone-floored dairy was down two steep steps from the kitchen and was half underground. The window was level with the ground outside and covered with a fly screen. Even on the hottest summer day it was always very cool indeed and in winter it felt like the North Pole. There was no refrigerator and eggs, butter, cream and milk etc. were all stored there. In one corner was a complicated machine called a cheese press. I never saw it in action, although my mother Isabella (always known as Cissie) Verity Eglin, née Ryder, said she had used it long ago. Around the walls were shelves formed from stone slabs where bacon was cured on beds of straw. Usually there were also sides of bacon and ham hanging from hooks suspended from the ceiling.

In another corner of the kitchen was a copper boiler which was only used when we slaughtered a pig. On those days, the whole back yard would resemble a charnel house – complete with dismembered pig and buckets of blood. On washing days, before we had a washing machine, it was done in a "dolly tub." This was a large zinc, barrel-shaped tub in which clothes were placed and then pounded vigorously with a "posser" which was a copper funnel on the end of a long stick. The "whites" had "dolly blue" added to the water. This was a small block of blue powder wrapped in muslin. It certainly did the job as well as Surf or Omo! A lot of starching was done for collars, pillow cases and sheets etc., the starch being mixed from a powder. There was also a "dolly cream" used for cleaning the net curtains. It also came in handy to rinse the prize sheep before a show to make their fleece a nice cream colour, along with dabbing black shoe polish on their noses!

The living room had an old-fashioned cooking range with an oven heated from the open fire by a system of flues. Mother did all her baking in this oven and said that it baked better bread than the electric cooker which arrived after the war. The smell of "baking day" lives on in my memory (this was usually Tuesday, as the washing day was Monday). Bread was kneaded by hand and placed in front of the fire to rise. Usually about four loaves of bread along with teacakes, buns, biscuits and pies etc. were baked at one go. There was also an "oven bottom" cake which was like a teacake with a hole in the middle. I used to like the slice with the hole in for some reason. An old grandfather clock ticked away in the corner of the room and a Delft rack filled with blue and white pottery stood against a wall. Propped up against another were some guns and a shepherd's crook.

Our farmhouse was actually a very attractive building. In those days it was covered with Virginia creeper which turned a glorious red in autumn. At the front was a large lilac tree, rambling roses grew over the parlour window and on the wall at the side was a "Dorothy Perkins" rose bush which flowered profusely all summer. The garden had peonies, marguerites, lupins and a variety of old fashioned flowers, mostly in verdant disarray as in the summer everyone was too busy to tend the garden. At the back of the farm was a garth or fenced paddock. One usually found the carthorse grazing there along with some geese, a few sheep or lambs and, from time to time, cows. Surrounding the farm were various outbuildings including another dairy or "cooling house." Milk was brought here from the milking sheds, cooled, filtered (or "siled") and measured into cans which were collected by Stockdale's transport and taken to the commercial dairies. There was a meal house for storing animal food (bran etc.), a couple of pigsty's, stables for two horses, haylofts and a garage. On the outskirts of Lofthouse we had more barns and milking sheds etc. Also, there were various outlying barns and hay storage lofts situated on the hillside above the valley. This valley or dale, as it is known, is where the Nidd flows before joining the Yorkshire Ouse, one of the rivers which ultimately forms the Humber. In days gone by, Nidderdale was one of the lesser known dales, probably because there was no through road other than a rough cart track which climbed steeply up the side of the valley, meandering north over the moors to before descending into Wensleydale.

During the Second World War, the village itself had probably no more than a hundred or so inhabitants. There were several outlying farms such as Blayshaw, High Lofthouse, Limley, Studfold and Thrope etc., but other than farmers or those connected with farming in some way, there was little other employment except for a few council workers who swept the roads and attended to the sewage plant. There was a shopkeeper cum postmaster, a publican and a vicar whose Manse was just outside Lofthouse. There may have been one or two people who worked down at Foster Beck Mill near Corn Close, just above Pateley Bridge, which was spinning heavy yarns e.g. Hemp for the twine and rope industry until 1966, but I have no recollection, for example, of anyone working in an office or a bank. To do so they would have had to travel to Pateley Bridge or even Harrogate. There were several retired men, widows and spinsters who lived alone. The women were probably alone due to the First World War, when many men perished. The main village street came to a dead end just above our farm, where a gate opened onto the cart track mentioned above. This road was impassable except for horse drawn vehicles or those of a more rugged type. During the war it was often used by army tanks etc. on manoeuvres which nothing did to improve its condition. In any case, in those days most people didn't have motor cars. Nowadays it is a tarmac road leading to Masham in Wensleydale and a popular drive for tourists.

Running off the main street were several flagged "ginnels," "snickets" or "alleys" depending on what you care to call them. There was a Wesleyan Methodist Chapel and at the back of the village shop cum post office was a building referred to as "the old chapel." It was used as a storeroom for the shop, but had chapel type windows and an organ gallery at the back. I remembering it being in a sorry state of disrepair. There was the village institute; the Lofthouse Memorial Institute was its full title (now the village hall). This consisted of a hall with a wooden floor, a billiard room/kitchen and ladies' and gents' cloakrooms. It had a stage with curtains and a piano.

In the middle of the wall to the rear of the stage (though I stand to be corrected here) was a monochrome portrait of a very stern looking Sir William Nicholson, a major landowner in the area. Wonderful concerts, dances and whist drives were held in the Institute Hall. Many took place during the war years, where a lot of local talent participated. Names that spring to mind are Walter Nettleton and Mrs. Hardy who sang "Madam will you walk" (they had a limited repertoire as this song was performed at every concert). There was also a lady of Indian descent (rumour had it she was from Bangalore), who was married to one of the Manning brothers from Thrope farm – see Wartime Recollections below. She sang very well and added a little eastern glamour to the proceedings. There were some evacuees from the East End of London who could tap dance. One evacuee family was especially talented. They were the Baldassares. Obviously the dad – who never appeared – must have been Italian, but the mother and children were very definitely East Enders. I felt sorry for them as they were given a barely inhabitable old cottage to live in for the duration of the war. They had very little furniture, but were a big, raucous and happy family who had the noisiest children ever. The normally quiet villagers were horrified by them, but they used to perform very well at the village concerts. Mrs. Baldessare had a very bad reputation. She chain-smoked, wore red nail polish and heavy makeup, dyed her hair ginger and, worst of all, she used to visit the pub, something that village women did not do. Rumour has it that on Victory in Europe Day in May 1945 she danced on the table in the Crown Hotel wearing a pair of knickers made from a Union Jack. I can believe it – she was that type of person! One of the daughters, Joyce Baldessare, started a class for tap dancing. She charged 6d (2.5p) per lesson and gave them in one of our haylofts which had been swept out. However, a new venue soon had to be found as apart from the noise disturbing the two horses' underneath, the floor was in danger of collapsing. We also had our school play in the Institute. I was a witch in a production of the "Spick and Span Stone" (a play by Enid Blyton) and wore a pointed hat made from black cardboard. I was very hurt that I could not be a fairy as my friends were prancing about in very pretty tulle blue dresses with tinsel trimmed wings attached, but in the end it turned out alright because my part was bigger.

After concerts or whist drives there was usually a dance. This could only start when the Crown Hotel closed as the "Midnight Follies", the dance band run by the Coates brothers, Billy, Lawrence and Raymond, were all in the pub getting suitably lubricated. The band consisted of Billy Coates on piano (he never used any music sheets) with Lawrence and

The Memorial Institute

Raymond on saxophone and drums respectively. It wasn't Glen Miller, but they could certainly make that old hall rock after a good "oiling" in the Crown. The dances were old time like the "Veleta" and "Palais Glide" etc., but the highlight of the evening was a set of the "Lancers." All the big farmers took part in this; dad, Tom Whitfield, the Moore lads etc. and it was really wild with the ladies being swung off their feet and showing a fair amount of Directoire drawers and suspenders! The floor was powdered with French chalk to make it slippery and I can still remember the sweet, sickly smell. It was very good for sliding on. Children were allowed to attend as a special treat. There were no baby sitters and these dances only took place very rarely. We made a thorough nuisance of ourselves by rolling billiard balls across the table until someone eventually stopped us, usually with a clip on the ear. Village ladies served refreshments like potted meat sandwiches; homemade Victoria sponge and good strong tea. There was no coffee and I certainly do not remember any alcohol. On New Year's Eve, the local policeman, a Scot named Jock Chalmers used to exchange his uniform for full Highland dress and pipe in the New Year.

People I knew in and around the village of Lofthouse were not smart or sophisticated, but plain country men and women. Some of them possibly never travelled further than Harrogate during their entire lives. The farmers were all well-scrubbed, ruddy faced and had their hair plastered down with water or Brylcreem. They wore what were probably pre-war shiny suits or rough tweeds and looked uncomfortable in a collar and tie. Ladies were usually in homemade dresses (courtesy of the Womens Institute sewing classes) and not wearing much make-up. Anyone who coloured their hair or painted their nails was considered rather "fast." Whist drives were held where prizes could be won. Mother once won a red coloured tin alarm clock which lasted for years and could wake the dead. These whist drives were very cut-throat affairs and if anyone wrongly trumped an ace, it was considered a serious matter. The WI also held their meetings in the hall and on one occasion I remember going to hear a talk by the novelist Naomi Jacob. I was fascinated because she dressed and looked like a man, but she did tell me that I was a "good little girl" for sitting still. Jacob wrote excellent novels about Yorkshire life, although they are now somewhat dated. She later emigrated to Italy and lived in Sirmione on Lake Garda and wrote about Italian life.

During the war years a class called "Make do and Menders" was run. Local ladies had to produce a new item of clothing made from an existing garment. For example, jerseys were unpicked and the wool was re-knitted; ladies dresses were taken apart and made up into something for children. I remember mother having a brown coat with a fur collar and kept hoping that one day I could swagger around the village boasting the fur collar. Alas, I had the coat remade, but without the fur collar. There was also a knitting circle where wool was allocated to the ladies who knitted scarves, balaclavas and socks etc. for the troops. Mother never seemed to be without a bag of endless khaki coloured knitting.

There were also cookery demonstrations by the WI and wartime recipes which made rations go further were part of this programme. Luckily, living on a farm, there was no shortage of food, but I can still remember the packets of dried powdered eggs that were used in cooking. Eggs were also preserved or "put down." This entailed putting eggs in large pails of waterglass (sodium silicate mixed with water was used as an egg preservation agent throughout the early 20th century). I don't know what it did, but they didn't go bad. We also ate a fair amount of rabbit meat which, although somewhat underrated today, is far tastier than chicken. If dad had a sheep that wasn't looking too good, he would slaughter it for us to eat, but this had to be done secretly as it wasn't legal. I must admit that during the war if we wanted spare parts for the tractor etc. a leg of lamb might be traded. This was the "black market." As mentioned already, we also slaughtered our own pigs, but half had to go to the government. I hated home cured bacon. It was preserved on straw in the dairy with saltpeter and was always very fatty and salty – ugh! There was a part of the pig which as children we always looked for. That was the bladder. It was dried out and made into a fairly good, but not so round football. During the war, although we had a sheep farm, we had to allocate some land (on government orders) to produce food. The water meadows near the river were the only part of the farm that was suitable, the rest being hilly. We grew oats, potatoes and swedes. As children we were given a week's holiday round about October for "Tattie scrattin" – in other words, digging out potatoes. We also received help with the harvest. This was done by a machine - I think called a reaper-binder - but not a combined harvester. It cut the corn and threw out sheaves. We then had to stand these up on end, four together to form "stooks" as they were known, so they could dry out whilst keeping the grain-heads off the ground. As the corn was being cut, and the binder moved towards the centre of the field, all the rabbits, rats etc. would be driven inwards. The farmers would then load their guns and wait for all the wildlife to dash out as the last few rows were cut. I couldn't bear to see the slaughter and made sure that I was far away when it happened. I also remember a rabbit that used to eat all the lettuces in the garden. One day I saw dad go for his gun, so shouted out of the bedroom window "run rabbit, please run" and it did! Dad wasn't too pleased. After the corn had been led home, the thresher used to come and separate the grain from the stalks. This was a monstrous great traction engine and we were never allowed near it. There were great big leather belts which drove cruel blades and made a terrible noise. The air was filled with dust and chaff and the peaceful village atmosphere was shattered for the day.

The village library was also run from the Memorial Institute. This consisted of two boxes of books which were changed periodically by the county library. We used to race up there after school on Mondays. Being an avid reader, I really loved it and what pleasure I gained from those battered, dog-eared books. I remember particularly "Milly-Molly-Mandy" whose adventures with Billy Blunt and her little friend Susan were a delight. I also read my way through all the Biggles stories (Captain W.E. Johns); Bevis and Mark (Richard Jefferies) and the Arthur Ransome books. I was lucky in that my sister Judith had lots of lovely pre-war books which were handed to me. Comics were not approved of – at least by mother, but cousins passed on Dandy and Beano. Dad was the first to read "Desperate Dan" in the Dandy.

Also during the war we had film shows sponsored by the "Ministry of Information." We were allowed to attend these. They were free and supposedly educational, but were interminably boring being (or so it seemed to a seven year-old) solely about machinery. I imagine the films were about the war effort. Later, some enterprising person introduced a monthly film show at the Institute. These were old films, but I remember seeing "Treasure Island" amongst others. We loved these shows as we rarely went to the cinema. In fact, the only films I remember seeing as a child were "Snow White and the Seven Dwarfs" and "The Wizard of Oz" which my sister took me to see in Harrogate. This was at the St. James Cinema, which was on Cambridge Street, but it closed in 1960. I also remember something called an "epidiascope" which my dictionary describes as an "optical projector giving images of both opaque and transparent objects." I think it was also referred to as a "magic lantern" and was often used at Sunday School.

Not far from the Institute was the local hostelry known as the Crown Hotel, run by Tom Bradley and his second wife Mary Jane (née Eglin), who was some distant relation on dad's side, although she was much older than him. Rumour had it that she was neither a man nor a woman – certainly she lived as a woman although she never had any children. Once, when she was sick, I went with mother to visit her. She was wearing a fancy lace nightcap which mother had made for her to cover her bald head. I recall that Mary Jane always wore a rather

The Crown Hotel

terrible ginger wig which looked as though it was made from coir matting or had been knitted by someone. She also had whiskers on her chin and a very peculiar voice. Maybe there was some truth in the above rumour. Actually, I should state, Mary Jane was a very nice person indeed. I used to do errands for her such as posting letters. She used to wait for me passing on my way home from school and give me peppermint cordial to drink and let me look at "Picture Post." Tom Bradley, on the other hand, was an inflated, pompous little man with a large moustache which he used to wax into two fine points. During the war Tom was responsible for air raid warnings. In the unlikely event of the Germans ever finding Lofthouse, he was supposed to walk up the village street blowing a police whistle. When all the danger had passed, provided he wasn't annihilated in the said air raid, he then had to walk up and down the street ringing the school hand bell. I only remember this happening once and I think it was a practice. However, it made Tom feel very important and any Germans would probably have died laughing at his pomposity anyway, so he served his purpose one way or another. After Tom's wife Mary Jane died, he married his barmaid Norah Bell in 1949 and a great celebration was held. Sadly, I was at boarding school (Ripon Girls High School) and missed it. The Crown always smelled of stale beer and had a dark and dingy tap room only frequented by a few locals. It was usually the same old crowd every night. "Crutchy" Kirkbright (so-called because he was disabled and used crutches); Ted Brown and maybe one or two of the Harrison brothers from Studfold Farm (Eli, Herbert or Jimmy). They normally had a couple of pints and played dominoes. I do not recall ever seeing anyone worse for drink except one Reg Lee, brother to Dinah Lee's (née Metcalf) late husband Norman who had been away playing with the village band and had to be driven home by dad. Reg insisted on beating his drum, which was on the back

6

seat next to me, all the way home. At the rear of the pub was a large garden which grew excellent rhubarb and as children we often had stomach ache from eating it raw (having stolen it of course – this was divine punishment).

Down the hill past the Crown was the disused railway station, complete with ticket office and platform etc. The railway had been closed since the completion of Scar House and Angram reservoirs, located further up the valley, when it was used for transporting material to the building sites. A spinster lived in a flat above the ticket office. The poor lady was disabled and couldn't speak properly or control her facial movements. She came in for a great deal of ridicule from us children as one of our games was to see how far we could creep up the steps before she came out and started swearing at us incoherently. We were awful, but then no television etc., we had to amuse ourselves.

Next to the station was the village school. What happy days I remember there. The school consisted of two classrooms, one for the little class (4-10 years) and the other for the big class (11-14 years). I went there when I was four years-old. Dad's cousin Nellie Eglin was our teacher. She probably never had a great deal of tertiary education, but she taught me everything that I have ever needed during my life. We learned reading, writing and arithmetic – but properly. All three were

The former Station House

drummed into us never to be forgotten. Each day started with us lining up in the school yard after we heard the bell. The youngest were in front and the oldest at the back. Then we marched into the big classroom for prayers. This was followed by bible study. We often had to learn psalms and great chunks of the bible off by heart. Arithmetic was next and we recited all our tables up to twelve times. This was followed by stones, pounds and ounces; yards, feet and inches; gallons, quarts and pints and even measurements in Imperial units like bushels, pecks, perches, poles and rods. We also learned to write properly, drawing pages of pothooks and round o's until we could do it perfectly. One thing stands out in my mind; Nellie taught not only me, but various cousins as well and we all have excellent handwriting which all looks the same! Nellie took us on nature walks down to Sandbeds, for example, a stretch of the River Nidd below the village. She made it all so interesting, but never stood for any nonsense and could give a good clout when necessary. She took us for P.T. as well. This might not seem unusual until I tell you that she had a severely twisted club foot and wore high surgical boots, one of which had a heavily built-up sole. Nellie always wore rather severe long dresses to cover her disability, but she could walk fast and run with us in spite of it. I remember that we had a maypole in one corner of the classroom and Nellie taught us to dance round it to music from an old wind-up gramophone. She must have possessed a great deal of patience as those ribbons used to end-up in terrible knots and she would have to undo them. However, we did a maypole dance one sports day and it was "all right on the night."

I remember Nellie teaching us girls to knit, sew and embroider. I wasn't all that good at knitting, but started off with a dishcloth described by mother as "more holy than godly." Then I graduated onto a pixie hood in shocking pink and brown, a pot-holder in blue and yellow and later a doll's vest of all

Lofthouse School

things. I always wanted to knit like Molly Burton, who lived at Limley (then later at Summerbridge) and sat on the back row of the class. She knitted a yellow Angora wool jersey and could do fancy stitches. During the war, we all had to have a rest at school during the afternoon covered by blankets made from coloured knitted squares. We were also given a spoonful of cod liver oil every day which we used to hold in our mouth and then spit out in the yard. At that time the school windows were covered with mesh to stop the glass shattering in the unlikely event of an air raid. On VE Day all the mesh was stripped off by the big lads and suddenly it all seemed so light and sunny as we had known nothing but gloom caused by the netting. Another thing that stands out in my mind is a dish of porcelain fruit which stood on the classroom window sill – I wonder whatever happened to it?

We also had a school nurse who visited from time to time. We were weighed, measured and our heads inspected for lice. As a well-fed, warmly clothed farmer's daughter, I did not really understand that in those wartime days food was rationed and some children from poor families were under-nourished and some actually had lice in their hair. I can remember rushing home and telling my mother that one or other of the evacuees had "bugs." My long hair was immediately washed in something that smelled awfully like paraffin and then being closely scrutinized and my hair combed with a small toothed comb until my head was sore. This happened for weeks until the scare was over – all this to loud protestations of course. The phenomenon seemed to coincide with an influx of evacuees from the East End of London. They were like people from another planet. For a start, we had a communication problem because we didn't understand the cockney accent and they couldn't understand our broad vowels. These children were much more street-wise than us, but were frightened of cows; didn't know our country games; didn't

8

know the names of flowers or birds; couldn't comprehend why there were so few buses and cars and wondered why there were no cinemas. Some of the them were obviously suffering a great deal. I remember one or two who used to wet themselves in class and one particular little girl who frequently became hysterical. We thought the evacuees were very strange indeed and on occasions the village children would "gang-up" on them. It all seems so cruel now, as they had been taken away from their parents and homes and placed into a strange environment and, of course, some of them would never see their parents or homes again. A few of them were billeted on outlying farms where there was no electricity and the host families were hostile to them. On the other hand, there were others who loved it and remained, grew up, married and are still living in the dale to this day. Some of the evacuees were very dirty and unwashed. Nellie used to go berserk because one of her idiosyncrasies was that all her pupils had to produce a clean handkerchief every day. Each morning before prayers she insisted that we all blow our noses. Woe betide anyone if they didn't have a clean handkerchief. I remember tearing a perfectly good one in half for my best friend Shirley Connall who had forgotten hers. The evacuees didn't seem to know what a handkerchief was and let their noses run or used a sleeve. Poor Nellie, she simply couldn't handle this at all and used to keep a supply of clean rags for them. (This handkerchief habit has stuck – I cannot get friends to understand why I won't use tissues!) Nellie also insisted on hair being tidy and socks being "pulled up." And if we swore at school, Nellie would take us into the cloakroom and wash our mouths out with soap and water – yes really!

I remember some of the farmers lads coming to school wearing poor clothing and clogs, but their garments were spotlessly clean, well patched and mended. I also remember them having to stay at home to help with sheep clipping, haymaking etc. The "kid-catcher" used to visit from County Hall as this was illegal, but there was no way of preventing it. Anyway, most of them have done alright for themselves. None of us looked particularly smart anyway, as clothing was rationed, and we all wore hand-me-downs and homemade items in any case. I was always eternally grateful to Auntie Katy, one of mother's cousins, whose husband was a Harrogate solicitor and father-in-law had been the Mayor of Harrogate and was known in the family as "Lady Bountiful." She made the occasional trip to the farm, passing on clothes from Zoe, Betty and Pamela. It wasn't because we were poor, but rather that everyone was in the same boat and clothing was in short supply. The coupons we had were needed to buy sturdy outdoor clothing for dad, good shoes (which we always had) and decent warm winter coats. All the rest didn't matter too much. It certainly made one appreciate and look after one's clothes and we were not allowed to hang them on the floor as my own children did – much to my horror. Also, Katy's children had some very smart outfits, most of which were totally impractical for a tomboy farmer's daughter. One pair of blue satin party shoes stands out in my mind. We always had a school party during the war. Mothers contributed cakes, sandwiches and home-made biscuits. My mother always made a trifle because we were the only people in the village with real cream. We played games like "blind man's buff" and "here we come gathering nuts in May" and pinning a tail on a donkey. I used to get very envious of my friend Shirley. On these occasions Nellie bent the rules and we were all allowed to wear our hair loose, i.e. not plaited. Shirley's would fall into beautiful long ringlets almost down to her waist, whilst mine, in spite of ministrations and a painful night with it in rags, persisted in hanging as straight as ever.

Dad used to supply the school with milk. It was delivered in a large aluminium can with a lid. In winter it was placed on top of the coke stove to warm it up. The milk was not pasteurised, tuberculin tested or homogenised in those days; it was straight from the cow, cooled and filtered, that's all. Goodness knows what sort of micro-organisms lurked in the milk, but no one got sick from it and there was always a good inch of cream on top. It used to fall to my lot to cart the can back home. It did seem big and heavy and I used to have to rest half way up Bradley's Hill (the steep section of road past the Crown Hotel) or take a short cut through Tom Watson's farm yard. This was hazardous, as we had to make sure his geese were not in the yard as they chased us. Another favourite pastime in summer only, was to see how far we could walk across the crust which formed on Tom's muck midden before it gave way and we sunk ankle deep in cow muck, or until Trissie Watson, his sister, came out and cleared us off.

THE CHARACTERS

Looking back, there were some really odd people living in Lofthouse. We knew who they were and they were accepted as being "eleven pence ha'penny to't bob." At the top of the village, where the road ended, lived the Horns. They had two sons, Raymond and Herbert. The whole family were devout Wesleyans, and Mrs. Horn ran a small Sunday School in the Wesleyan Chapel which I went to on occasions. In fact, the reason I was stopped from attending, was that she frightened me to death with tales of hellfire and brimstone and, sinner that I was, it was running rather close to the bone. I remember being terrified of dying in my sleep after Mrs. Horn had told a particularly hair-raising story of people who went to bed and didn't wake up. I used to arrange myself lying dead straight, hands clasped across my chest, so that if the call came during the night, I should be suitably ready!

There used to be wondrous harvest festivals at the chapel, and then perhaps two days later, we would sell all the donated produce for charity at a mock auction. These festivals were lovely. The chapel was decorated with produce and sheaves of corn and flowers. There were huge cabbages and vegetable marrows; magnificent turnips and swedes; potatoes with their jackets scrubbed clean and a profusion of

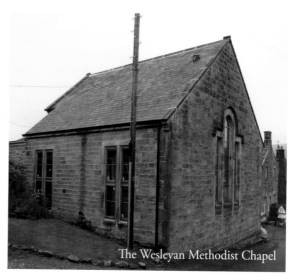

The Wesleyan Methodist Chapel

10

chrysanthemums and Michaelmas daises (the festivals were usually held in late summer or early autumn). I remember roof raising renditions of "Come Ye Thankful People, Come" and "We Plough the Fields and Scatter" to the accompaniment of Mrs. Horn on the harmonium. Herbert Horn was in the Salvation Army and was always interrupting sermons during the service by exclaiming "Praise the Lord" whenever the preacher said something that he agreed with. The last time I saw Herbert was at Skipton railway station when I was at school. He was working as a porter. Raymond, the other brother, was rather more reasonable and I believe he went to Cliff College at Calver, near Sheffield, to train for the ministry.

Opposite the Horn's farm was a stately Victorian building called Gladstone House which faced down the village street. It was at one time occupied by my best friend Shirley Connall and her mother, the father was away fighting in the war, and we spent many hours there playing in the porch which no longer exists. That was when we weren't shouting derogatory comments at Herbert Horn and then ducking behind the wall. In front of the House stood the First World War Memorial (Victory Memorial to commemorate the end of WW1). It had a tap and water trough, but I believe flowers are grown in it now. Just along from Gladstone House and in the corner of a flagged yard lived a man called Billy Parkinson. I think he was a retired blacksmith. He used to wear a Homburg hat and was of a fairly smart appearance, but his house was a bit of mess. I don't remember a Mrs. Parkinson.

Next to the Chapel, on what was known as the Chapel Flags, lived another old man – Ted Brown. He always wore a flat cap and a muffler and I often wondered why he didn't walk straight when he came home from the pub. There again, there was never a Mrs. Brown. Just around the corner, next door to Ted, lived Florrie Andrews. She was

Gladstone House with road to Masham on left.

slightly older than the rest of us village kids and lived with her mother who was a widow and called Lily Wardman. Lily was the only woman in the village I knew who ever went in the pub. Florrie had a magnificent vocabulary of swear words and she also told us a great deal about the facts of life. Nearly all of us were forbidden to mix with Florrie, but as she went to the same school it was difficult to avoid her. Next to her lived Granny Williams who also used to get drunk and swear like a trooper. She had a vicious bull terrier which she let off the lead one day and it attacked my pal Roland Coates, biting his face.

Behind the Post Office, down what was known as the "back alley," lived an old lady called Miss Pratt. She wore Victorian clothes and looked like the lady pictured on

CHR

Gilbert, Cissie, Christine and Judith Eglin

Policewoman in West Riding Constabulary

Haymaking at Haver Close Farm in 1930's. Upper right Gilbert Eglin, bottom right daughter Judith

LOFTHOUSE

Please drive carefully

TINE

the prints of the "Delicious Mazawattee Tea" adverts. We used to visit her because she was always good for a biscuit or two. Opposite Miss Pratt lived "Owd Lizzie," the main character of the village. Lizzie was almost bent double with what must have been some awful arthritic condition or spinal disease. She lived in almost indescribably filthy conditions. Indeed, the inside of her house, walls, floor and ceilings, were totally black from smoke. The house was filled with an assortment of junk and Lizzie appeared to like it that way. In this day and age, it would not be allowed. Social workers would have moved in and taken her to some pristine home where no doubt she would have died in misery. Mother said it was rumoured that Lizzie had been "in service" somewhere when she was young, though it was hard to imagine her in a neat maid's uniform. One wonders what had happened in her life to make her turn into a recluse. At one time she was taken ill and removed to hospital where she was obviously well looked after and cleaned up. She arrived back in the village as a dear little white haired old lady and nobody recognised her. In a few days, she was back to the Lizzie we all knew, dressed in her rags with a sack around her shoulders, her face ingrained with dirt and wearing a greasy old hat. I expect she received some sort of pension, but spent her time going from farm to farm scrounging food and milk and collecting gossip. At Christmas she would visit all the farms and be given Christmas Cake etc. I believe that when she died, numerous tins of mouldy, decaying cake were found in her house.

There was also another Lizzie - Lizzie Graham - and she lived at Stean with her brother who was known as "Lang Bob" because he was very tall. She wore a strange assortment of clothes consisting of layers and layers of skirts. She also possessed a big hat which had a piece of stocking top hanging from the front to keep flies off. This Lizzie could often be seen walking between villages. She had a particularly long striding gait and would talk to herself as she strode along. Lang Bob used to ride an old bicycle and was a strange character. Mother used to say they were of gypsy descent. I was a little bit scared of Lang Bob. He used to loom up across the fields and I would give him a wide berth. This was mainly because of his weird appearance which resembled that of a large wild scarecrow.

As previously mentioned, there were quite few single ladies living alone, perhaps due to husbands being killed during WWI. There was a lady called Susan who used to work as a cleaner at the school. She was a miserable old lady if ever there was one. We used to steal gooseberries from her garden until the village bobby caught us. He gave us a quick swipe with his rolled-up cape and told us to go when she was not at home like he did! Then there was old Miss Schooler who was stone deaf. Our favourite trick was to sneak up behind and tap her on the shoulder which made her nearly jump out of her skin with fright. Miss Schooler was Scottish and we always got lovely shortbread from her. Another old lady lived in a cottage next to the farm. This was Miss Emma Carling, a cousin of dad's. She was notable for wearing Victorian clothes right up until she died in about 1950. She even wore the long pantaloons, which caused us great merriment. We knew this because she used to hang her washing in our paddock at the back of the farm. Another family were the Leadbeaters; Mrs. Leadbeater and her three sons Hilton, Joseph and Guy. Hilton and Joseph did not do anything and Guy was the only one who did any sort of work – he repaired bicycles.

I noted on a previous visit to Lofthouse in 1988 that most of the cottages which are referred to have disappeared. The village is full of strangers now and I wonder if anyone remembers these old characters. We were never told to keep away from them. Indeed, we were never warned about strange people at all. We knew who the odd characters were; they were just that, odd, eccentric, harmless people and none of them broke the law. We would often harass them and call names after them, but otherwise we accepted them as part of the community. The worst that could happen was that we learned several choice Anglo-Saxon swearwords! I should like to add here that there were many perfectly normal decent people living in the village too!

THE VILLAGE SHOPS

There used to be two shops in Lofthouse. The first was the Post Office/General Store, which was run by old Mr. Oddy during the war. I remember vaguely there was also a Mrs. Oddy, but she died. Her husband was then pursued by Susan Harker who used to do his cleaning. Rumour had it that she was after his brass, but he never did marry her. Old Oddy used to keep the shop open all hours, each and every day. There was never a time when you could not enter the shop because it was closed. The lads used to go for cigarettes after half past ten at night when the pub had closed. Everything from a pin to an elephant was sold, or so it seemed. I can remember going with a pint jug to collect vinegar, which was drawn from a barrel like beer. Paraffin was pumped from a large drum. I also recall that butter and cheese were in big blocks and cut with a wire. Sugar came in sacks and was measured out carefully on brass scales with weights. Sometimes it was wrapped in a twist of paper rather than put into paper bags. There were big tins of biscuits; one didn't buy a packet of them, one had them weighed out on a scale. For a few pennies we could also buy bags of broken biscuits from the bottom of the tins. In the window were big jars of sweets. We could buy aniseed balls and glacier mints; Nuttall's Mintoes; sticks of liquorice; humbugs and some large sweets we called "gob-stoppers" which changed colour as we sucked them. There were wooden crates containing bottles of pop, though I seem to remember that there was only red pop and lemonade. We could also purchase a delicious drink called Dandelion and Burdock – whatever happened to it? We used to walk to the village rubbish dump and collect bottles, before washing them in the beck and taking them to old Oddy in the shop to collect the deposit. Then we could buy another bottle of red pop with the proceeds! Sweets were rationed during wartime and I remember cutting coupons out of all the family's ration books and taking them to Oddy, where I intended to buy about a pound weight of sweets. Oddy wasn't taken in and promptly marched me and the coupons back home. It was a good try though! Those were the days – a postage stamp for an ordinary letter was two pence ha'penny.

Two of my friends, the Price twins, lived in a council house and I could never understand how they could go to the shop and buy things without money. Old Oddy just wrote something in a book. I can remember wanting to buy lemonade, and then thinking that I didn't need cash, because the Price twins bought stuff without money. I was told that "We didn't do things that way." The twins' father was the local council employee who cleaned the roads. He had been in the army and he died just after the war from pneumonia. Valerie Price later married Jack Challis and lived at Hazel Close. Oddy had a ginger and white cat called Topsy which used to sleep on the potato sack and a large Labrador dog called Duke. The dog would lie in the middle of the street and would not move for anyone; cars had to drive round him.

The other shop was run by Mrs. Baker, with no Mr. Baker ever in evidence. This was a strange little triangular shaped shop and the window was filled with imitation bars of chocolate made from wood and covered in paper. This imitation chocolate was in the window for as long as I can remember. In fact, they were so old that the paper had curled up exposing the wood underneath. Mrs. Baker sold a few packets of cigarettes and pop. She used tea to colour her hair. We knew this as she would often appear with tea leaves in her hair. She lived with her sister, a Mrs. Dick Coates – no relation to the other Coates family in the village. Once again, no "Mr." in evidence. This lady was like a character out of a Somerset Maugham novel. She never did any work and spent the day trailing around the garden in chiffon outfits wearing a big hat and long dangling earrings. She could also be found wandering along the riverside, in her trailing lace and chiffon, talking to herself. On the outside of Mrs. Baker's shop were large enamel signs advertising Brooke Bond Tea. These were very good targets for throwing stones at. It made a pleasing sound when they hit and was guaranteed to bring one or other of the ladies out to chase us away.

THE SEASONS

Each period of the calendar had its specific activities, as well as the seasonal farm work, and there were also children's games played at different times during the year. In Spring we usually waited for the first lambs to appear and hoped that there would be some orphans to be bottle fed and raised as pets. Often, lambs born in the snow would be brought back to the farmhouse in a comatose state. They were wrapped in a sack and placed on top of the cooking range and given milk and brandy out of a baby's bottle. This used to revive them in no time. If a sheep had lost a lamb, and a lamb had lost its mother, the dead lamb would be skinned and the skin placed over the orphaned lamb. In this way the lamb would take on the scent of the dead one and be fostered onto the ewe. During the Great Snow of 1947 (see below) we had nine orphans, all given German names by our POW Werner Jürss, who was working for us on the farm. At feeding time, they would be at the back-door bleating to be fed. Werner organised the lambs in a typically German way as they were stood carefully in line for their bottles.

We were always on the lookout for the first spring flowers to appear, usually Coltsfoot followed by primroses and we could gather great bunches of them from the banks of the beck near How Stean Gorge. There always seemed to be so many, and however many we picked, there were lots still left growing. After lambing time, but before haytime, sheep were always gathered in from the moors for clipping. This was usually late May or early June when the weather was warming up, and the woods were full of bluebells. Our sheep and lambs were all gathered in the paddock at the back of the farmhouse. The bleating was deafening. However, all the sheep eventually found their offspring and quietened down. When this was done, any strays were sorted out. Dad could recognise all his sheep and knew if any of them

16

did not belong to him. I must confess that they all looked alike to me. The strays were returned to their rightful owners. Though once dad found Jack Harker trying to sell two of our sheep at the auction. Jack was the father of Freddie Harker who married Dorothy Verity's sister Mary – and they were still living at Stean in 1991. Most farmers helped each other out at this time, and I remember that the Walker lads from Blayshaw (brothers to Judith Walker at Hebden), used to come down to help with the clipping. Evered Walker once put a sheep tick on me, and they cannot be removed easily. I never forgot it, and never really trusted him again, though the poor soul has now passed away.

Sheep were clipped by hand in those days and the fleece was put on trestle tables and rolled into what can only be described as balls of wool, before being tied round with the tail. Wrapping fleeces was very good for the hands, because of all the lanolin in the wool. These fleeces were stuffed into and then sewn up in hessian sacks before they were transported to the woollen mills in Bradford. I also seem to recall another activity where we collected bits of sheep's wool which had caught in the hedgerows and on fences, but it's very vague and hard to remember a specific time it happened. After the sheep had been clipped, they were marked – ours had a black cross on them (made with tar) and a red mark made by "reddle" a dialect term for a substance called red ochre. I hadn't heard that word anywhere else except in the dales until I came across it in Thomas Hardy's "Return of the Native." I quote from the book, "The traveller with the cart was a reddleman – a person whose vocation it was to supply farmers with redding for their sheep. He was one of a class rapidly becoming extinct in Wessex…" That was written in 1912 so obviously we were very backward in Yorkshire as we were still using it!

Once clipping was over, it was time to start preparing for haytime. Machines were brought out, oiled and the blades sharpened. Hayrake's were given new wooden teeth, and scythes were sharpened with a stone. In the early days of WWII, we had horses to pull the machinery – Dinah and Blossom – but later a tractor was acquired which made life easier. Any machinery needing a repair was taken to the blacksmith's forge at Pateley Bridge. The blacksmith was called Mr. May and it was a really exciting, wonderful forge with bellows and anvils and great hammering which sent sparks flying everywhere – sadly a concrete bus station now stands on the site. Mr. May sometimes visited the village to shoe the carthorses. On those occasions I can remember the irons and shoes being heated in the kitchen range and banged into shape on what must have been some sort of portable anvil. Old Dinah, the horse, was none too keen on the shoeing business and would frequently lash out with a good strong kick or two at anyone who ventured too near. Mr. May used to wear a leather apron and was obviously well trained in dodging the hefty hooves of a massive Clydesdale. Actually, Dinah was probably one of the most intelligent, but cantankerous horses ever. She would not do anything that she didn't feel like doing. If she decided to stop in the traces whilst pulling a cart, nothing would make her move, nothing. One night, she decided that her stall was not to her liking and proceeded to kick it down. We moved her to another and all was well. Dinah could also open most gates, and if she wanted to go walkabout, would either kick open the gate, knock down a fence, or, in one case, leap right over it. She would wander round Lofthouse in the evening eating prize dahlias and lilac bushes and anything else she fancied. Later she would come clip-clopping up the village street at all hours of the night. She was a law unto herself and impossible to keep confined anywhere. However, the only time I ever saw dad near to tears was when she had to go to the "knackers yard" at an age of about thirty-two years.

In June, the Bell Festival was held at Middlesmoor. This was started in 1868 when the Ring of bells was first installed in St. Chad's (I was fortunate enough to attend the centenary on 15th June 1968). On Festival day, we all had to have a new outfit. We then used to line up at ten o'clock and walk in a procession to the church, led by the Lofthouse and Middlesmoor Silver Band, with dad playing the drum or one of the Basses. He was the only bandsman not to wear a uniform because there was never one big enough to fit him. The church service was then held and afterwards we would have a sports day with three-legged, egg and spoon, and sack races along with other old-fashioned games. There were also traditional stalls and crafts like flower arranging (wild flowers) etc. Then there would be a communal tea in the village hall and later usually a whist drive and dance for the adults in the evening. This was the big event of the year. I remember one particular Bell Festival when I was running in a race and tripped and fell. As the sports field was usually used for grazing cows, I managed to land right in a cow pat. My new dress was covered and it was all over me too. I went to Aunt Hannah's (they had the Middlesmoor Post Office) to be put in the bath and then had to borrow a dress from Dinah Lee which was miles too big. It really ruined my day.

The start of haytime was usually in late June depending on the weather. I must say that it did seem better weather then, but perhaps I don't remember the rainy days – I'm sure there must have been some. The grass in the meadows was long and lush with an abundance of wild flowers and herbs. I understand since then that a lot of the wonderful plants have been killed off by insecticides and artificial fertilisers. In those days, the only fertiliser used was muck from the cow sheds produced during the winter months when the cows were under cover. The meadows were cut with a mowing machine that had long cruel blades. This was pulled by Dinah the old horse. The edges of the fields were cut by dad using a hand-held scythe, as the machine could not be used too close to the stone walls. Nothing was wasted. After a couple of days in the sun, the hay was turned by hand using rakes. This was very hard work and we were all roped in. We used to get badly blistered hands from the raking.

The best time was when the "drinkings" came. I was usually sent to fetch them from the farmhouse, a fairish walk, and brought back the food in big baskets covered with cloths. We used to have homemade sandwiches, cake and teacakes along with big bottles of tea and sometimes homemade barley water. We also used to eat what dad called "Fly pie" which was a pasty containing currants and not forgetting the inevitable Victoria sponge cake. Everyone would sit and relax for a few minutes and dad would light up his pipe. We were able see what was happening on the other farms in the dale – who had cut which meadow and who was ahead with their haytime. I could usually find a few field mice to play with, or perhaps some birds' nests in the hedges and, of course, the two border collies who were always in attendance. Looking back, ham and tomato sandwiches have never tasted better.

When the hay had been turned and dried on both sides, it was then "dashed" or "strewn" using a hay tedder with big spikes which tossed the hay into the air and completed the drying process. Now came the time to "get" the hay. The dried grass was raked into windrows and then swept into big piles which were great for jumping in. When it had all been swept up, it was formed into "pikes." These were stacks of hay, but built in a special way so that they didn't collapse. They had to be just right, and as children we were set on the pikes to trample the hay down and compact it. The pikes were "topped off" into a point and sometimes, if it was windy, a rope was made from twisted hay and the top was tied on. When all the fields had been harvested in this way, it was time to lead the pikes home. This was done originally on what was called a "pike cart" which was a flat-bottomed trailer with a winch attached. A rope was placed round the pike and the cart was tilted to an angle of about 45 degrees. The pike was then winched onto the cart and tied down. As children we used to ride on the back of this cart during the "leading" of hay from field to barn. In later years, a tractor drawn cart was used, which held up to three pikes, whereas the old pike cart only held one. Once at the barn, the hay was forked by hand into the hay mew through a "forking hole" - a trapdoor – which was usually pretty high up on the side of the building. Dad would be outside and maybe mother and the two German POW's inside. At the rate dad worked, those inside were usually swamped with hay and had to call for him to slow down. The children had to work inside the hay mew, trampling down the loose hay. This was in fact a far from an idyllic job – it was hot, dusty and dark in there. There was a special way of making a mew so that it didn't collapse and had a straight edge. Dad always insisted that it was done correctly. It was hard work, but we had a lot of fun. One of my happiest memories is after we had finished haymaking for the day, maybe nine or ten o'clock in the evening, being allowed to ride on the back of old Dinah all the way back to our farmhouse. She was usually lathered in sweat and still in her full harness. Her back was like a table top and I used to cling on to her mane. Those were lovely summer evenings; the smell of hay and all the cows waiting at the gate as milking time was long overdue. I wax nostalgic.

After haytime, we started to cut bracken from the moors to be used as "bedding" for our cattle in winter, though I understand that this is no longer done. It was tiring work and the bracken was often carted from the moors by horse and sledge as the terrain was very rugged. In the early war years, I remember that dad and the farm hands used to go out and dig peat. There was a shortage of coal, and peat seemed to be the answer. It was cut into squares or sods and then stacked up to dry. When the peat was completely dry it was light and had the same texture as a block of polystyrene. It was carted home and stacked in an outside shed. During winter it was used as fuel. As the peat burned it threw out more heat than coal and did not leave any ash except a fine white powder. I don't understand why it is not still used today, as it is clean burning and would not cause any pollution. I suppose the problem is that digging out peat can be hard work.

On the "glorious twelfth" of August, the shooting parties would head for the moors at the start of the annual grouse shooting season. Local lads usually went along as beaters to drive the birds out of the heather and normally there was a good "bag." Most of the shooting parties came from towns, and there were always a few MP's and other "gentlemen." As children we used to earn a few shillings by opening gates for them. Tom Heard from Halfway House (between Lofthouse and Middlesmoor) used to take a horse and cart loaded with all their food and drink. Afterwards, there were always several brace of grouse being "hung" in the dairy until they were "ripe." Aunt Madge Eglin, who lived at Dovenor House in Middlesmoor, used to take in some of the visiting gentlemen. There were three sisters running Dovenor – Lily, Madge and Nellie (the schoolteacher). Lily was a widow, and Madge and Nellie never married. Lily was disabled with arthritis but did all the baking whilst sitting at the kitchen table. Her baking was superb and her sponge cakes were out of this world. Madge was very fat, jolly and did most of the hard work. I should add here that Madge was something of a character. She was overweight and always wore dresses which were far too short. She would bend over to poke the fire and show all her britches! This used to embarrass Reverend Champion, the vicar, a great deal as he was a frequent visitor due to Nellie running the Parrish Council. The vicar was Mary Champion's father – I remember her from Ripon Girls High School. And it was Nellie (in her retirement) who did most of the organising at the house. I used to help them out during the school holidays when they were getting old. I have eaten at some of the world's best restaurants, but have never had food like they could make.

As Christmas drew near, there were always extended preparations. The house had to be cleaned from top to bottom. I believe that this is an old Viking custom and a way of banishing evil spirits and has probably been handed down through the generations. Dad was always dispatched to bring back some holly and mistletoe (the real stuff), but he would never let on where it grew. I think it was probably somewhere in the woods going up the valley towards Thrope, as that was the general direction he disappeared in. Dad also used to bring us a real Christmas tree as they grew in profusion in the dale. The owner of the estate where we farmed was killed at Dunkirk and his son was too young to inherit and manage the land. Therefore, the woods had been left to go to seed. The trout breeding dam in the river was also abundantly filled with fish which were there for the taking. I think the gamekeeper was absent too, away somewhere in the war.

The Christmas cake was always baked round about September or October so that it had time to mature. During the war, dried fruit and other ingredients were hoarded throughout the year so that there would be enough for a cake. We usually cooked a goose for Christmas dinner, which I understand is also a Scandinavian custom. Though one year we decided to eat a very bad-tempered cockerel (rooster) because he had been attacking people who walked through the yard. However, when it came to execution day, we granted him a reprieve. He was a very fine bird and we were quite fond of him and he did keep the more undesirable elements from trespassing. In fact, the cockerel kept everyone from trespassing, such was his ferocity.

The fat from the goose was carefully saved and used for rubbing on chests and chilblains (a similar custom is observed here in South Africa, with fat from a buck). When Christmas Day dawned, we could usually hear the bells from the church up at Middlesmoor ringing down the valley. By mid-morning the village brass band, led by the aforementioned publican Tom Bradley, would come and stand around the fountain in front of the farmhouse and play carols. Sometimes we had a white Christmas. I can remember waking up knowing that there was snow outside even though we still had blackout curtains. There was always a certain quietness when everything was covered. I could never wait to get out and into the snow and quite often would be soaking wet before breakfast. Now was the time to bring out the sledge, prevail on dad to sand and oil the runners, and then tramp to Tom Watson's field. It had a steep bank and a gate at the bottom which we would open so that we could sledge straight through it and across the road. This was not dangerous as there was no traffic in those days. The village streets were cleared by a horse drawn snow plough. Although it pushed the snow aside, it did not clear the roads as well as today's modern ploughs. Most vehicles had chains fitted on their wheels to help deal with the winter conditions.

Sometimes at Christmas we would have a party in the evening. I was not allowed to stay up for the party, but spent a lot of time at the top of the stairs watching the proceedings below. It was mostly relatives who were invited, Uncle Carling and Aunt Hannah who kept the Middlesmoor Post Office; Auntie Cis (Dinah's mother); Lily, Madge and Nellie (Dad's cousins) from Dovenor House; one or two farmer friends and sometimes the vicar and his wife. One of the games they played was a form of "pass the parcel" where the forfeit was to dress up in whatever was in the parcel. Imagine the vicar in granny's bloomers! They seemed to have a hilarious time. Mother used to make quite a big spread and there was always a trifle in a large enamel dish. I had usually stuck my fingers in the cream a few times during the day. Everything was homemade with things like home fed ham, mince pies etc. They would all have a drink, but I don't think that there was much alcohol consumed. For a start, drink was scarce and expensive in war time. I can remember mother making some kind of egg-nog (or egg-flip; alcohol mixed with beaten egg and milk) which had a small amount of brandy in it, but that's all. On New Year's Eve the custom was for the man of the house to let the New Year in. Dad used to go out before midnight and return bringing back several objects through the door after the clock struck twelve. I cannot remember them all, but one was coal, another was usually the highly indignant cat who had been disturbed from its warm bed in the barn, but the rest escapes me.

During the war years, children's toys were unavailable. I can recall being given a knitted golliwog, and also aunts who used to knit us scarves and gloves. We received a lot of second-hand books which had been passed around, but generally I think we really appreciated our gifts and took care of things so they could be handed on again later. I can remember that every Christmas I had to clear out books and toys that were finished with and pass them on to Christine Suttill who was a distant relation. She was disabled with spina bifida and unfortunately her father had been killed in the war. As stated, we didn't get very much, but were taught to value and take care of our possessions and then share with those less fortunate.

OTHER MEMORIES

I was fortunate enough to pass my eleven-plus exam which earned me a place at Ripon Girls High School where I was a boarder. I hated leaving home, but as I was fairly running wild in the countryside, it was probably a good thing. Whilst away at the school we lived in the attached hostel which was run by a certain Miss North, who had been a nurse in WWI. Miss North must have been about fifty years old. She had red hair worn in a severe bun and never wore make-up. She always had sensible lace-up shoes, a plain tweed coat and a hat stuck squarely on her head.

She tried her best to make ladies out of us. We had to go for walks after school in a "crocodile" (walking in pairs). We always had to wear our hats and gloves and make sure that shoes were clean and socks were pulled right up. There was no rowdyism and we were not ever allowed to walk past the boys' school. Food was still short after the war and at school mealtimes we were given a carefully measured square inch of butter and about (I think) two slices of bread. We ate very plain food; fish pie and a dish called "monkey meat" (corned beef or tinned meat), shepherd's pie and other meals which I can't (or don't want to) remember. Sometimes there would be cake, perhaps about twice a week. Breakfast and high tea were taken at the hostel; lunch was at the school. On reflection, it was all very institutionalised.

I think my godparents, Harold and Hilda Waring, deserve a mention. Hilda was a member of the Verity family from Gildersome, near Leeds. Harold was a very cultured man. He had been the chief engineer at Joshua Wilson and Sons' Mill in Leeds and his great interest was classical music, mostly church music - Bach and the like. How on earth Harold and Hilda ever got together I shall never know. Hilda was small and round and very extroverted. Her interest in music consisted of banging out choruses from Gilbert and Sullivan with the loud pedal on and usually with a cigarette in her mouth. They never had any children, but devoted themselves to the children of others. Hilda was always doing good work for someone; looking after the sick; knitting and sewing for church bazaars and generally helping out. During haytime, she would turn-up at the farm complete with a large apron and mountains of food, overseeing the catering for the day. When I used to stay in Leeds, she would organise myself, Marjorie Prince (her niece) and Wendy Baguley (a neighbour) with a picnic, and put us on the tram to Batley, Pudsey or Roundhay Park for the day. She would tell the conductor where to drop us off and what time we had to be back. In fact, she could tell anyone what to do and get away with it. I remember sitting in Betty's Café in Harrogate for tea. In those days my greatest desire was to devour cream horns. There wasn't one on the plate, but Hilda asked all the waitresses until they found one. I always loved to visit the News Theatre which was located outside Leeds City station, next to the Queens Hotel in City Square, to watch cartoons (the News Theatre opened in 1938 and closed in 1979). Hilda would take me and patiently sit alongside whilst they played over and over again. They used to own a little Morris Eight. Harold was a very careful and cautious driver, but Hilda thought nothing of grabbing the steering wheel whilst saying something like, "come on Harold, it's left here" and turning the car suddenly, leaving her poor husband shocked. In her later years, she took to wearing a wig. One day her sister Mary said that she thought Hilda had the wig on back to front. Hilda agreed that it was indeed on back to front because she had been lighting a cigarette from the gas fire and set the front of the wig alight!

Another person who I should mention is Gladys Jinny Brown (Miss Brown). She was my music teacher and lived at a house called "The Nook", adjacent to Granny Ryder in the village of Ramsgill, approximately two miles down the dale from Lofthouse (Granny Ryder lived at The Old School House next to The Yorke Arms, and was the housekeeper for local artist Stephen Denison). Miss Brown or Gladys Jinny, as she was always known to us, shared the house with her aged mother who was a disabled, but rather dear old soul. If I had been particularly good, I was allowed into the front room to meet her. Miss Brown was a magnificent pianist and music teacher. She was highly qualified, as the many certificates which lined her staircase demonstrated. She also had a roll of honour on top of the piano, naming all her pupils who had passed their exams. Nobody had failed; most had passed with honours and quite a few with distinction. She believed in teaching theory and had a notebook in which remarks were written to one's parents every week. If one's playing was not up to scratch, it was duly noted, with strict instructions that more practising was required. Miss Brown was a little sparrow like woman with thin, claw like hands. She used to wear bracelets which dangled and rattled when she played. A ruler was kept handy in case the wrong notes were hit too many times. Should that occur, the unfortunate pupil was likely to receive a strong rap on the knuckles - I wonder what the child psychologists would think of this? Anyway, I passed with honours three times, damaged psyche or not!

After the lesson was over, I had to wait for the bus back to Lofthouse. Usually I went to Granny Ryders' next door (or if she was in the Yorke Arms, I went there!) but after Granny died, I had to remain at Miss Browns. She had a large Mickey Mouse Annual for me to read (how do I remember all this trivia?) Sometimes she used to ask if I would like her to play something on the piano and choose which piece I wanted to hear. So, being a rotten kid, I looked through all the music until I found something that appeared to have lots of black with Hemi-demi-semiquavers and ask her to play it. I am sure she knew what I was doing, but it never bothered her and she trotted out all sorts of obscure concerti with no trouble at all! She was also the official pianist for the Womens Institute and gave a magnificent rendition of "Jerusalem" on a monthly basis. Incidentally, her lessons cost two shillings per hour (and often went on longer than a hour). One Christmas, I remember that Miss Brown's mother knitted me some puce coloured gloves with flowers embroidered on the back (trivia again!) The pop songs of that era were "Galway Bay" and "Goodnight Irene," but Miss Brown would not allow any such songs to be played. When she found them in my music case folded inside "Smallwood's Piano Tutor" and "Czerny's Selected Piano Studies" there were ructions. Other girls who went to Miss Brown's for tuition were Sheila Rispin (from the Waterhouse at Gouthwaite) and Florence (Totty) Smith. Poor Gladys Jinny Brown died aged 91 in 1991 (though she looked old in the 1940's!) and I recall seeing her grave in Ramsgill Churchyard.

WARTIME RECOLLECTIONS AND OUR POW's

At this stage, I think I should write about some more of my wartime recollections. Although I was only two years old when WWII started, by the end I was seven and very impressionable. I have already referred to Tom Bradley and the somewhat primitive air raid precautions, but the local Home Guard also needs a mention. They were known as the LDV - Look, Duck and Vanish! As stated, there were only a few men left on the farms, and these were folk like dad who were running their farms plus the local men they employed. I might add that most of the farm men were those who were either too old or unfit (mentally or physically) for the services. One family that springs to mind were the previously mentioned Harrisons from Studfold Farm (who later lived at a cottage in Lofthouse). They had three sons; Eli, Jimmy and Herbert. Both Eli and Jimmy worked for dad at some point or another.

Eli was considered a bit daft. However, the story goes that when they called him up for the Home Guard, he was given a gun and told to do some target practice. Eli managed to shoot the windows out of the Memorial Institute and, of course, was rejected. He told the tale in the pub afterwards, saying that he knew what he was doing, but didn't want them to think he was a good shot as he might be called up for the army (how daft?) I happen to know that he was a very good shot as he used to go potting-off rabbits on a regular basis. His brother Jimmy was also a bit silly. He was working for us once, with dad and I playing "I Spy." Jimmy came up with "I spy something beginning with F." Well, we struggled for ages until we just had to give in. It turned out to be "Thread" (Fred!) Apart from the Home Guard, there was also the Royal Observer Corps who had a hut out on the moors near Northside Head above Middlesmoor. I don't know how much observing was done, or, in fact, if there was anything to see, but I did hear that they had a pretty good card school!

Next was the ARP – Air Raid Precautions. Dad was a member of the ARP and was supplied with masses of protective clothing, including waterproofs, leggings, wellies, tin hat, gas mask and a stirrup pump, plus an endless amount of webbing and buckles. I can remember one call out and by the time we had got him into all his gear, after much cursing and grumbling, the all clear had been given. One day, a huge army truck drew up in front of the farm and out stepped a very smart officer with a small tin in his hand. Apparently, he asked dad if he had any anti-dim, to which dad, with his usual wit replied "no" and he hadn't any uncle dim either. Anyway, they had driven all the way up from Harrogate to deliver his anti-dim which was supposed to stop his gas mask from steaming up! (the tins contained an anti-dimming cloth which was rubbed onto the moistened eyepieces) I cannot ever remember dad putting on that uniform again for the whole of the war. It was never collected afterwards and is probably still hanging up in the "balks" somewhere.

As stated earlier, the family who lived at Thrope farm during the war were called Mannings. There were two bothers and a sister. The two brothers were conscientious objectors, or so they said. Most of the local farmers claimed that their objection was because they didn't like work. The family were almost completely ostracised and never received any assistance from the other farmers who had no time for them.

I remember the army arriving on the moors to undertake manoeuvres several times. We village kids were straight into the army camp making a nuisance of ourselves, climbing on tanks and Bren gun carriers and wandering in and out of the tents. Dad used to supply the officers with milk and eggs and I can remember a crowd of them sitting down to a home-cooked "tatie" or rabbit pie. Food was rationed, but I think mother and dad considered this part of their war-effort.

One cold and wintery morning, dad woke up to find the fire brigade from Summerbridge, the nearest fire station, standing outside the farm round the fountain. He went outside and asked what was up and learned that they had been out all night on the moors extinguishing incendiary bombs. It was a habit of Luftwaffe bomber pilots to jettison their payloads on the moors on their return from cities or perhaps when they were lost I suspect. These bombs would set the peat on fire and it burned for weeks. The firemen had been up the dale to see what they could do, but having travelled as far as they could, realised that the fire, which could be seen for miles, was actually over towards Jervaulx Abbey in Wensleydale and therefore completely out of reach for them. They had got thoroughly soaked and frozen. Dad invited all of them in for breakfast. Later, round about Christmas, a truck arrived at the farm with a huge box of groceries. The firemen had all collected from their own rations and given them back to mother in gratitude. Now wasn't that nice?

After the war had ended, we were desperate to find farmhands, and so the authorities allocated us two prisoners from the POW camp at Ripon. They were called Werner and Otto. Initially they were brought by truck every day, but as they didn't arrive until after eight in the morning, it was no good for us, especially at lambing time, when sometimes help was needed all night. So, we were given permission for Werner to live at the farm. At last I had a brother! What a smashing chap he was. Werner could not speak a word of English, but after a while he became a member of the library! He had been a baker's apprentice in Germany and the Gestapo (or whoever) had arrived at his work one day and marched him off to join the army. He hadn't even been able to go home and tell his parents. He had seen action on the Eastern Front and taken part in the invasion of Russia. His unit had reached as far as Smolensk, where they were frozen in. According to Werner, even the petrol froze. He was billeted with a Russian family for a while and said they all slept on top of the stove. Later he had been wounded in the arm. Unfortunately, lice had infected the wound and prevented it from healing properly, so he doubted if he could ever go back to the baking trade. However, we had him treated and his arm was eventually properly healed. Werner must have been with us for about three or four years. He was definitely on the farm during the harsh winter of 1947.

Werner soon became one of the family. At Christmas he always received presents from us and Auntie Hilda, bless her, would bring him something every time she came to visit. "Where's our Werner?" she would say. He was honest, trustworthy and hardworking, something we were not used to with English farm labourers. He had a niece, Ilsa, the same age as me and we used to write to each other, with Werner translating the letters. I used to hope my elder sister Judith would marry him, but that was strictly "not done!" He started courting Janet Kirkbright, but eventually he had to return to Germany because his sister's husband had been killed and he had an obligation to support her and their children. Also, he was supposed to have a girlfriend called Elfriede back home. I still have a carved wooden parrot that Werner made for me. He went back to Eastern Germany and I often thought I should have tried to contact him. He used to write regularly to mother and ask for things that were unavailable like sewing cotton, torch batteries and some tinned food products. Suddenly the letters stopped and we wondered if the Russians (more likely the Stasi) had prevented him from any further correspondence.

When the prisoners first arrived on the farm, they used to bring their own food from the camp. It consisted of dry black bread and not much else. Mother used to throw it into the pig bucket and both were fed from our table. As she said, you couldn't expect them to do a day's work on those rations. I remember Colonel Somebody or another from the camp arriving to check on the two men. He complained that we were treating them too well; after all, they were POW's. Mother said, "Look here, they are somebody's sons, and if they were mine, I would want them to be treated well". There's no answer to that, is there? Nevertheless, we weren't too popular with certain people. For example, some of the other farms had POW's living in too and we used to let them meet once a month in the front room, just to get together with their own countrymen. It was illegal, as they were not supposed to be out after dark, but they would otherwise have had a miserable time. I recall one POW named Joseph who worked for Stoney's at Summerstone, further up the dale, and another Otto who went to George Beecroft. There were also two prisoners, Kurt and Walter, who were taken on by the estate and lived in a little cottage in Middlesmoor. Kurt was massive and mother used to say, "I would have been scared of him if they had won the war" whilst Walter was short and fat. They were the type of jovial Germans one would see at a beer festival for instance. Both were employed as painters and decorators and came to paint our farmhouse. Kurt would be up a ladder painting the gutters whilst Walter would be stood at the bottom. Nothing unusual in this, except that they sang operatic duets the whole time – that is when they weren't arguing about something in German. It was like a music hall turn. The cottage where they lived in Middlesmoor was in the row that faced the church, the end one next to where Dinah Lee lived. The cottage was very dilapidated, so between them they renovated and repainted it. I can remember going inside to see the living room. A huge tree had been painted on one wall and on its branches were painted the most exotic birds. I expect they did it to pass the time. Their painting was very good and they also did some lovely wood carving. I rather suspect that they were from southern Germany where many of the houses and chalets have decorative carving and their outside walls are painted with murals (known as Lüftlmalerei).

One point worth mentioning is that the Germans were the most spotlessly clean people I ever met. Werner and Otto would strip off to their waists in the back yard and scrub themselves clean before they ever entered the house. They also never set foot inside with their mucky boots on. Mother used to wish dad would do the same! A barber came from the POW camp in Ripon once a month to cut their hair and we all used to receive a free haircut at the same time. The barber was quite effeminate with very wavy hair which had clearly been styled. All the prisoners wore jackets with "POW" on the back. Werner used to say it meant "Prince of Wales." They were supposed to keep their prison issue on all the time, but we found him some civvy clothes to wear. We also gave him pocket money – all strictly illegal. He took to farming very well and dad always said he was the best farmhand we ever had. Of course, he didn't belong to the farmers union! All in all, the Germans got on very well with everybody. They seemed to integrate into village life quite easily; they were allowed to visit each other and I don't remember anyone having any real animosity towards them. It broke my heart when Werner had to return to Germany. I lost a friend and the nearest person to a brother I ever had. When the time came he cried, we all cried, and I hope that whatever happened to him, his memories of us are as fond as ours are of him.

Finally, another recollection is that of a Messerschmidt Bf 109 being shot down over Masham. I can remember being taken to see it and being surprised at how small the aeroplane appeared to be. It was all fairly boring and I was much more fascinated by the fact that the crash was supposed to have blown an old lady out of the bedroom window and she landed up a tree in her nightie. I was also taken to see the army engineers building a bridge across the river. They laid rows of planks across small boats or pontoons. When they were attached all in a line, the troops could walk across. There was also a large naval mine placed in the village (presumably made safe with the explosives and detonator removed). We were encouraged to buy savings stamps and stick them on it. When it was full, it was supposed to buy a battleship. Thinking back this might have been one of the "warship weeks" when towns and villages across the country were asked to raise funds for the navy and then "adopt" a ship.

ON REFLECTION

Looking back, on the whole, I think the generation of war children were far better adjusted than today's youngsters. This is only a personal observation, but children who suffered the trauma of being evacuated from their homes and separated from parents did not seem to become maladjusted and grow up into criminals. They went through far more trying experiences than today's children. Kids still living in London used the Underground to shelter during air raids. Food was short, clothing was rationed and there was no television. Generally, and I emphasis generally, those growing up in wartime conditions seem to have been better able to deal with life's challenges without the help of psychiatrists and social workers. Perhaps the answer is that they were taught to <u>live</u> and survive on their own and be responsible for themselves. Personally, I do not ever remember being bored or unhappy. We were not allowed to sit around doing nothing. If we were seen to be loafing or at a loose end, a job was soon found for us. After school, we had to change into old clothes and wellies which were suitable for working in the farmyard. I was allocated certain regular chores which included feeding chickens, calves, dogs, horses and, in winter, cows. There was also firewood to be brought inside for the next day and maybe a one mile walk uphill through the fields to the shop at Middlesmoor. I was able to knit and sew simple things by the age of six. I made a dress totally by hand before I was ten years-old. It was dreadful, and it was never worn, but I learned to hem, running and fell stitching (whatever that was), sew and darn – this being before the days of disposable socks! So, at an early age I was expected to sew on buttons or stitch up a broken seam. I also had to help with the ironing. There were four of us in the family when my sister Judith was home from Ripon Girls High School, where she was a boarder, plus my ancient and senile aunt Miss Emma Carling and one live-in farm hand. Mother was expected to do all the cooking, cleaning, washing and most of the ironing etc. We slaughtered our own pigs and mother always said she used everything except the squeak. Bacon and ham were home cured, there were marvellous pork pies and brawn, and we made our own butter. Oh yes, that was a soul-destroying job – churning butter! As kids we thought up our own entertainment and got ourselves into quite a lot of mischief doing it. I can remember several of us trying to navigate the River Nidd in someone's "dolly tub." Just looking at the river now, why didn't we all drown? We ate wild crab apples until we were sick. During the war we collected rose hips from the wild dog rose and were given one penny per jar collected. We went carol singing at Christmas and maybe raised half a crown each. This was big money and would buy a really good hardback book. Tragedies did happen. Brian Sykes was drowned in the sewage beds; Roland Coates was savaged by a bull terrier; Yvonne Price and I became trapped in a lime kiln and had to be pulled out – this was no tragedy, it was rather fun actually. Perhaps I was one of the luckier ones. We had a good home and were very well fed. We never went short of food or clothing. We always had a motor car and I used to be taken on more visits than most children. I used to spend holidays in the big city – Leeds – with my godparents and was occasionally taken to pantomimes, films etc. and Uncle Harold took me to see my first performance of the Messiah in Leeds Cathedral. Dad was on the District Council and mother was in the Womens Institute, Mother's Union and a member the Parish Council. They both belonged to the Conservatives! So, all in all, I had a very happy, fortunate and adventurous childhood living at our Lofthouse farm, located in the beautiful Yorkshire dales.

THE GREAT SNOW OF 1947

Finally, I want to add a few memories of a severe winter we experienced in our village, which also affected the whole of the UK. From the third week of January 1947 there was a great blizzard which cut us off from the rest of the world for several weeks. The snow ended up being very deep and covered the windows on one side of the house where it had drifted. Many farmers ran out of fodder for their sheep and supplies were dropped from aeroplanes. We lost relatively few sheep. Dad seemed to sense when the weather was going to be bad. I remember there were friends visiting us on the night it started. After we had watched them leave in their car, dad put on what we used to call his "big boots" and heavy outdoor clothing and out he went with the two sheepdogs. He did not return until the next morning, but had brought as many sheep as he could find down to the lower pastures. By this time the snow was thick on the ground and I think we eventually lost about sixty sheep. We had an incredible old blind sheepdog who had really been pensioned off from farm work, but she was one of the two he took. Although she could not see, she would go and stand on the snow where a sheep was buried and just bark. The dog saved many lives! Lennie Woodrup at Scar lost almost his entire flock, and after the snow had gone, they dug pits to bury the carcasses, covering them with quicklime. During the great freeze, I remember several of us from school walking up towards Scar to see how far we could get. We went through the disused railway tunnel (now bricked up) which had icicles like pillars stretched from the roof to the floor. It was like something out of a fairy story. Some children couldn't reach the school at all. I was not so fortunate, as after a few days, the undaunted Nellie was able to get through. She travelled by horse and sledge from Middlesmoor, accompanying milk cans and post on their way down the valley to Pateley Bridge. So lessons re-commenced as usual. It would have taken more than the blizzard of the century to keep Nellie away. There was still snow on the hills in June of 1947. Unfortunately, I later contracted measles and was unable to attend school. I went out on the moors with dad for some fresh air to aid my recovery.